Where Animals Live

Swamp Animals

By Katie Buckl

2   I see alligators in the swamp.

I see pigs in the swamp.

 I see herons in the swamp.

I see water buffalo in the swamp.

 I see egrets in the swamp.

I see dragonflies in the swamp.

I see snakes in the swamp.

I see frogs in the swamp.

I see wallabies in the swamp.

I see butterflies in the swamp.

I see owls in the swamp.

I see hippos in the swamp.

Word List

vocabulary words

swamp	buffalo	wallabies
alligators	egrets	butterflies
pigs	dragonflies	owls
herons	snakes	hippos
water	frogs	

73 Words

I see alligators in the swamp.

I see pigs in the swamp.

I see herons in the swamp.

I see water buffalo in the swamp.

I see egrets in the swamp.

I see dragonflies in the swamp.

I see snakes in the swamp.

I see frogs in the swamp.

I see wallabies in the swamp.

I see butterflies in the swamp.

I see owls in the swamp.

I see hippos in the swamp.

CHERRY BLOSSOM PRESS

Published in the United States of America by Cherry Lake Publishing Group
Ann Arbor, Michigan
www.cherrylakepublishing.com

Photo Credits: © Srinivasan.Clicks/Shutterstock, cover; © Kurit afshen/Shutterstock, title page; © Dennis W Donohue/Shutterstock, 2; © Gary Rolband, 3; © David Havel/Shutterstock, 4; © The Escape of Malee/Shutterstock, 5; © asharkyu/Shutterstock, 6; © Mike Truchon/Shutterstock, 7; © Kichigin/Shutterstock, 8; © Kurit afshen/Shutterstock, 9; © Michal Pesata/Shutterstock, 10; © Andreas H/Shutterstock, 11; © Wirestock Creators/Shutterstock, 12; © nataliatamkovich/Shutterstock, 13; © Photoongraphy/Shutterstock, 14

Note from publisher: Websites change regularly, and their future contents are outside of our control. Supervise children when conducting any recommended online searches for extended learning opportunities.

Cherry Blossom Press is an imprint of Cherry Lake Publishing Group.

Library of Congress Cataloging-in-Publication Data

Names: Buckley, Katie (Children's author), author.
Title: Swamp animals / written by Katie Buckley.
Description: Ann Arbor, Michigan : Cherry Blossom Press, [2024] | Series: Where animals live | Audience: Grades K-1 | Summary: "Swamp Animals showcases animals found in a swamp environment, including animals like alligators and egrets. Uses the Whole Language approach to literacy, combining sight words and repetition. Simple text makes reading these books easy and fun. Bold, colorful photographs that align directly with the text help readers with comprehension"– Provided by publisher.
Identifiers: LCCN 2023035090 | ISBN 9781668937631 (paperback) | ISBN 9781668940013 (ebook) | ISBN 9781668941362 (pdf)
Subjects: LCSH: Swamp animals–Juvenile literature. | Swamp ecology–Juvenile literature.
Classification: LCC QL114.5 .B83 2024 | DDC 591.768–dc23/eng/20230911
LC record available at https://lccn.loc.gov/2023035090

Printed in the United States of America

Katie Buckley grew up in Michigan and continues to call the Mitten her home. When she's not writing and editing, you'll find her gardening, playing music, and spending time with her dog, Scout. She has always loved books and animals, so she's a big fan of this series.